THE ESSENTIAL COLLE

BALLE

GOLD

P. 18
P. 70

Published by:
Chester Music Limited,
8/9 Frith Street, London W1D 3JB, England.

Exclusive Distributors:
Music Sales Limited,
Distribution Centre, Newmarket Road, Bury St Edmunds, Suffolk IP33 3YB, England.
Music Sales Corporation,
257 Park Avenue South, New York, NY10010, United States of America.
Music Sales Pty Limited,
120 Rothschild Avenue, Rosebery, NSW 2018, Australia.

Order No. CH68772
ISBN 1-84449-609-0
This book © Copyright 2004 by Chester Music.

Compiled by Michael Ahmad and Heather Ramage.
Music engraved by Note-orious Productions Limited.

Printed in the United Kingdom.

Your Guarantee of Quality:
As publishers, we strive to produce every book to the highest commercial standards.
The music has been freshly engraved and carefully designed to minimise
awkward page turns to make playing from it a real pleasure.
Particular care has been given to specifying acid-free, neutral-sized
paper made from pulps which have not been elemental chlorine bleached.
This pulp is from farmed sustainable forests and was produced
with special regard for the environment.
Throughout, the printing and binding have been planned to ensure a sturdy,
attractive publication which should give years of enjoyment.
If your copy fails to meet our high standards, please inform us and we will gladly replace it.

www.musicsales.com

CHESTER MUSIC
part of the Music Sales Group

London/New York/Paris/Sydney/Copenhagen/Berlin/Madrid/Tokyo

An Introduction to Ballet History, Music and Composers

People all over the world have always needed to express life and emotion through dance, originally in the form of spontaneous movement accompanied by the voice. So when did dance begin to develop into the lavish spectacle of technical feats, usually accompanied by an orchestra, that we know and love today? Outlined below is a brief history with reference to the ballets, music and composers featured in this book.

The idea of ballet started around 500 years ago in the private courts of European royalty, mainly French and Italian, the latter being responsible for spreading this art form around Europe. Dance was seen as part of early Italian opera, which accounts for why the word "ballet" finds its origin in Italian ("balli" or "balletti" meaning dances). As well as the principle composer of the opera, a second composer was usually employed to write for the brief, simple dance parts where male and female dancers wore cumbersome costumes, heeled shoes, and moved with elegantly turned out feet to renaissance music. In 1581, Le Ballet Comique de la Reine (The Comic Ballet of the Queen) was performed at a French court. The queen, Catherine de Medici, danced in it herself and it is thought to have been the first real ballet.

Dance then moved to the public theatre, still only seen within opera based mainly upon mythical stories. Gluck's 'Dance of the Blessed Spirits' from *Orfeo* (1762), is a well-known later example. The dances in these operas were only performed by men, as it was then considered improper for a woman to dance in public – a contrast to the seductive female roles from modern ballets such as *Sheherazade* and *Bolero*!

In 1661, Louis XIV, who danced himself, founded L'Academie Royale de Danse in Paris. This was the first establishment of its kind and explains why ballet terms are in French. The face of ballet changed in 1726 when dancer Marie Camargo caused a stir by shortening her dress and performing daring leaps when she stood in for an absent male dancer and thus set the trend for women to be as spectacular as men.

In 1832, the first romantic ballet, *La Sylphide*, was performed, in which Marie Taglioni danced exquisitely on "pointe" (in soft shoes) and in 1870, Marius Petipa, director of the Imperial Russian Ballet, introduced a different format of ballet where the story line was not as important as the "divertissements", which were developed to show off the dancers' skills and were accompanied by wonderful music, some of which you will find in this book of selected ballet pieces. The music and dance for "divertissements" are often inspired by a celebration or dream. For example, the 'Waltz' from *Swan Lake* sets the mood for Prince Siegfried's birthday and Christmas is the theme for *The Nutcracker*.

Choreography or music – which comes first? It could be either. For example, Tchaikovsky composed specifically for *Swan Lake*, *The Nutcracker* and *Sleeping Beauty* in collaboration with the choreographer, but *Rosamunde* (Schubert) and *Les Sylphides* (the first ballet without a story, originally called *Chopiniana* in 1907) were choreographed to music already written by the composer. Ironically *Swan Lake* was first choreographed by Wenzel Reisinger in 1877 and subsequently failed! It only became the best loved ballet of all time when Petipa re-choreographed it in 1893. Some roles, such as 'The Dying Swan' (1907) were created for a particular ballerina – in this case, Pavlova.

The music from *Don Quixote* (1869), *Pineapple Poll* (1951) and *La Fille mal gardée* (1828), all reflect humour and tenderness – the 'Clog Dance' from the latter is well-known for the hilarious "en travestie" (cross-dressing) role of pantomime dame, Widow Simone. A more serious recurring theme for ballet/opera is the legendary Faust and his relationship with the Devil – one of the most recent being *The Damnation of Faust* (Berlioz), staged by the Paris Opera in 1964.

Delibes' 'Hungarian Czardas', Borodin's 'Polovtsian Dances', Dvořàk's 'Slavonic Dances' and 'The Can-Can' (Offenbach's theatre music is frequently used for ballet) are examples of how music from different countries is often incorporated. Dance can also reflect political situations, e.g. *Gayane*, from which the 'Sabre Dance' is taken, celebrates Socialist Realism (Stalin expected art to echo his policy of rejecting the bourgeoisie and extolling the lives of the working class) and includes Armenian folk music.

Some composers are noted for their influence in the dance world. Adolphe Adam is famous for his atmospheric music and the development of "leitmotif" (theme tunes for the main characters which delicately change every time they appear). Delibes, who studied under Adam, also used leitmotifs in *Coppélia* (1870). His beautifully orchestrated melodic score for *Sylvia* (1876) is considered to be a great masterpiece. Minkus is well-known for his love of Austrian dance music; even if the waltz is ill-suited to an Indian temple or a peasant dance, nobody seems to care! This is evident in the music from *Don Quixote*, an extract of which can be found in this book. Prokofiev, arguably the most popular dance composer of the twentieth century because of his ability to convey raw emotion, satire and humour, wrote for many ballets, including *Romeo and Juliet*. A return of interest in Ragtime music in the 1970s resulted in several ballets being choreographed to Joplin's compositions – the most notable being *Elite Syncopations* (1974).

Jayne Ramage
2004

Pas de deux

from Giselle

Composed by Adolphe Adam

Andante grazioso

Danse des Sylphes

from The Damnation of Faust

Composed by Hector Berlioz

Moderato

mp *gracefully*　　　　*sim.*

gradually dying away little by little - - - - - - - - - -

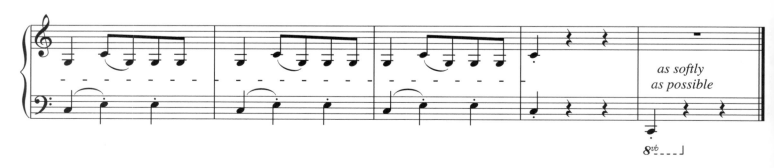

as softly as possible

Theme
from Prince Igor

Composed by Alexander Borodin
Completed and orchestrated by Nicolay Rimsky-Korsakov & Alexander Glazunov

Andantino

Czardas
from Coppélia
Composed by Léo Delibes

Valse Lente
from Coppélia
Composed by Léo Delibes

Pizzicato
from Sylvia
Composed by Léo Delibes

Waltz, Op.18

from Les Sylphides

Composed by Frédéric Chopin

Vivace

Nocturne
from Les Sylphides

Composed by Frédéric Chopin

Slavonic Dance No.8
from Slavonic Dances
Composed by Antonín Dvořák

Allegro molto

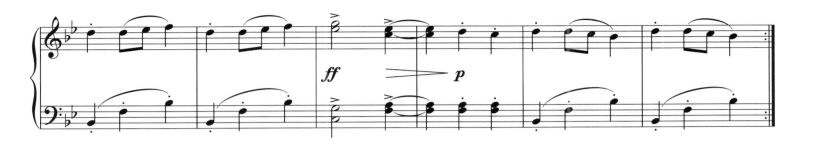

Dance of the Blessed Spirits
from Orfeo

Composed by Christoph Willibald von Gluck

Lento ♩ = 84

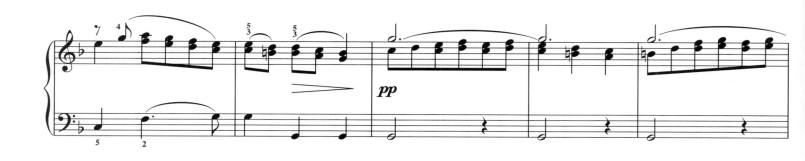

Clog Dance
from La Fille mal gardée

Composed by Louis Joseph Ferdinand Hérold
Arranged by John Lanchbery

(wood block or tap on piano)

Dance of the Priestesses
from Aida

Composed by Giuseppe Verdi

Elite Syncopations

Composed by Scott Joplin

Not fast

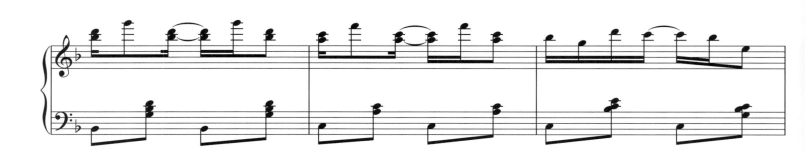

Saber Dance
from Gayane

Composed by Aram Khachaturian

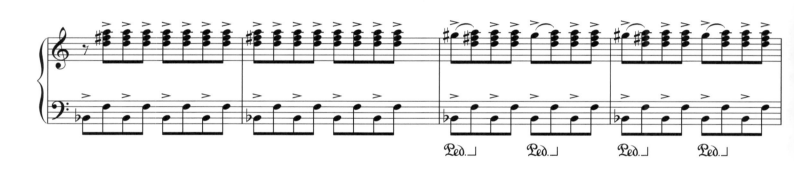

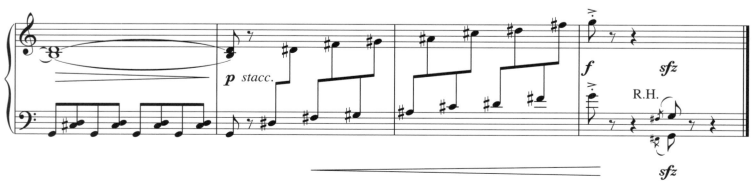

Entrance of Kitri and Basilio

from Don Quixote

Composed by Léon Minkus

Tempo di marcia ♩ = 160

Aragonaise
from Le Cid

Composed by Jules Massenet

Valse
from Cendrillon

Composed by Jules Massenet

The Can-Can
from La Gaîté Parisienne
Composed by Jacques Offenbach

Allegro

Dance of the Knights

from Romeo and Juliet

Composed by Sergei Prokofiev

Tempo I (Allegro pesante)

The Young Prince
and the Young Princess

from Sheherazade

Composed by Nikolay Rimsky-Korsakov

Andantino quasi allegretto ♩. = 52

Bacchanale
from Samson and Delilah
Composed by Camille Saint-Saëns

The Dying Swan

'The Swan' from Carnival of the Animals

Composed by Camille Saint-Saëns

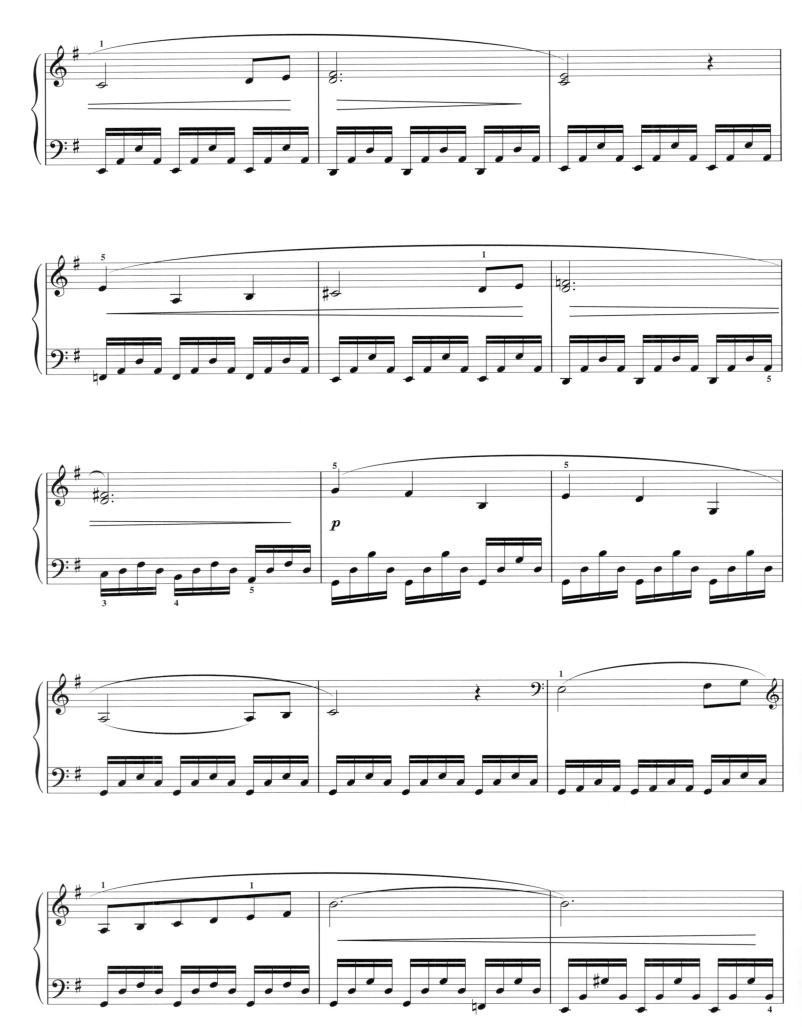

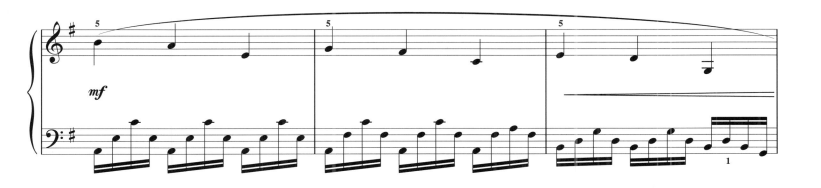

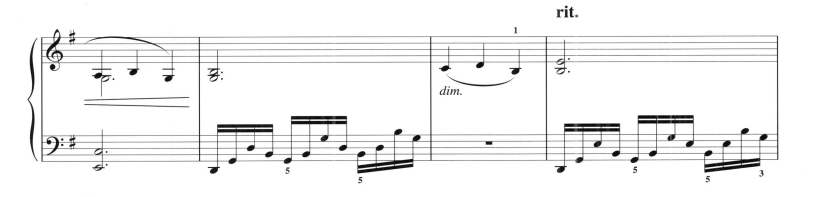

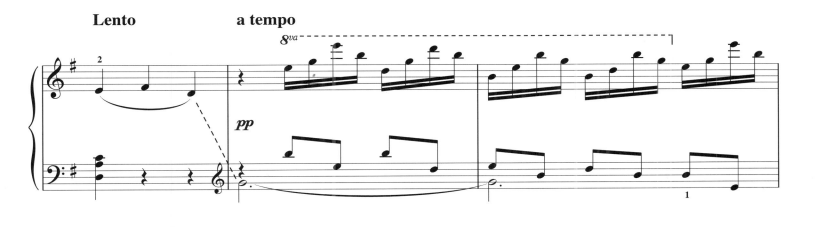

Grand Finale

from Pineapple Poll

Composed by Arthur Sullivan
Arranged by Charles Mackerras

Entr'acte
from Rosamunde

Composed by Franz Schubert

Dance of the Sugar Plum Fairy

from The Nutcracker

Composed by Pyotr Ilyich Tchaikovsky

March

from The Nutcracker

Composed by Pyotr Ilyich Tchaikovsky

Tempo di marcia

Danse des Mirlitons

from The Nutcracker

Composed by Pyotr Ilyich Tchaikovsky

Dance of the Cygnets
from Swan Lake
Composed by Pyotr Ilyich Tchaikovsky

Theme
from Swan Lake

Composed by Pyotr Ilyich Tchaikovsky

Waltz
from Swan Lake

Composed by Pyotr Ilyich Tchaikovsky

Tempo di valse

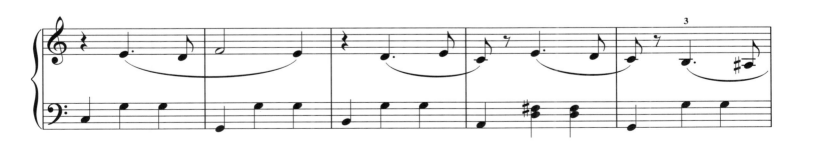

Waltz
from The Sleeping Beauty
Composed by Pyotr Ilyich Tchaikovsky

Fantasy Overture
from Romeo and Juliet
Composed by Pyotr Ilyich Tchaikovsky